MW01254210

THE

HAIRY

LOLLIPOP

AND OTHER POEMS

THE
HAIRY
LOLLIPOP
AND OTHER POEMS

BY DAVID WHITE

EDITED BY GEORGE CAMPBELL
MCDADE
SELECTED BY LINDA M. WHITE
COVER BY MATTÉ

Clevis Hook Press

Rochester, New York

Books published by Clevis Hook Press

Light at the End, The Jesus Poems
by Lyn Lifshin

Homeless Chicken Wing Tour - Poems
by Tony Nelson

Out of a Vale of Tears, In the Fullness of Time
by Dorothy Nowak Smith

Before Jazz
by Rick Petrie

Copyright © 2012 David E. White

FIRST EDITION

PRINTED IN THE UNITED STATES OF AMERICA

ISBN: 978-09821718-4-4

Clevis Hook Press

355 Spinnaker Lane
Webster, New York 14580
buckdavster@gmail.com

PRE-NATAL POSTURING

THE POSTCARD I PROMISED

Entering your eyes I gaze
and roam about your brain.

What thoughts have we here?
And how am I to read them?

Some are like billboards,
prominent but likely insincere.

Others poor half-discarded things
whose value you little suspect.

The ruts are deep and smooth,
the unexplored plateau inaccessible.

At night I visit fellow explorers around the campfire
Silence mostly, then some fantastic story.

Wish you were here.

HERE AND NOW

At the start
before I forget
before I am forgotten

I want to
thank someone
for letting me know
the only place
in Rochester
to buy a
spring binder
is the RIT Bookstore.

I need to thank someone
for preparing me
for sticker shock,
with his classy
therapeutic eyeball for detail
telling me at RIT
the spring binder
is called a
thesis binder.

Too personal,
too local,
references
become a thicket,
a massive snarl
of tether treads
holding words down
in the here and now

preventing them
from rising
into the ether

shining with a light perennial
—did I get that right?—
it is "perennial"
like the plants, right,
not eternal like the flame?

If this poem
be a flame
let it burn:
with simple combustion
we offer up not the self
which always was nothingness

but the pseudo-self
that so distracted me
and you and all of us,

offered up a sacrifice
to Hermes (and all the gods)
but Hermes I say because
unless I've got my facts wrong
it is Hermes who this moment
is within smelling distance

of our vapors,
the vapors of
the here and now tonight.

My method,
these methods,
are unexpected
as when a pearl
with 1/1,000
lithium salt
is brought
into a flame,

the red line of lithium appears,
but the naked eye notices
only the yellow light of sodium;
it sees no red at all.

Cut the tethers?
No.

I'm saying we need
to take seriously
here and now
the Buddha may simply
have been wrong,

we need to consider
in all seriousness
the nature of the self
and of our knowledge,
we need to ask who here is
and why poems go wrong

we need to consider
the objection to using
poems for money,
trying to use poems as money,
the way Vachel Lindsay did,
the way Pete Seeger did,

the problem is not
they misused poetry

but that important poems
got lost because
the owners did not care
for them properly.

CHILDHOOD

HAPPY

I knew someone
who on his birthday
went into the woods
as close as possible
to the moment of birth
and waited in patience
for the new year of life,
knowing that year, like
its siblings, would need
care and attention, but
most of all a chance to
grow old on its own.

THE MOTHER'S INFLUENCE

Looking back it is easy to miss a mother's influence.
The little fingers of memory cannot grasp the first few years.

Then complaints and prohibitions overshadow readings and healings.

A mother's influence is more like the sun among the planets:

Aligning, warming, and only rarely eclipsed.

MOTHERS OUGHT TO FINISH WHAT THEY START

Conceived in a tent
pitched by permission
on a millionaire's estate,
fed Dante for lunch,
scolded mercilessly
for some imagined insult
to relatives so eccentric
they would not know
a fart from a kiss,

allowed to climb tall trees,
swim in hidden lakes,
collect every manner
of insect dead or alive,
mix chemicals and keep
them in unlabeled bottles,
play foolish tricks on Grandma,
but never allowed to strike
my brother no matter
even with entire justice
and fairness and only
as a last resort,

descended, the only word for it,
from a long line of genetic defects
whose words were poems of denial;
whose lives were carelessly constructed
prose pieces trying to be patient
with the whole lot of coloreds, Jews,
homosexuals, and Catholics
but pressed for time to get out
the unabridged fulmination against
the WASP establishment,
which included anyone
with a higher degree
or willing to sit still for poetry
more recent than Tennyson.

Given my long-standing effort
to run away from home
and Mother the most aggressive
of my trackers,
getting herself to Africa,
moving in with me
until I agreed to come back
home and attend law school,

it comes as a surprise to no one
and a delight to some
to learn I have the requisite legal skills,
when we leverage Mother's holdings,
to allow me to buy a small company town,
with everyone in the town an actor
free to ad lib.

The townspeople are simple
folk with no experience
at leaving home, desperately
in need of a mother,
and here I have
a perfectly good mother
for which I no longer have a use.

Whatever got ensouled that night
in the tent, is not me;

doubtless I was not the first
of the family to keep chemicals
in unlabeled bottles

no one can live
as recklessly
or as close to nature
as we did
and not expect accidents.

SHED IN MIND

Again and again I return to the shed we played in,
our cathedral, parliament and laboratory.

The pure memory of broken glass, tortured insects
and cities made of sawdust is nailed to a moral frame.

Termites, wind and time took our shed;
Ted rebuilds it—in stories to his kids.
(They don't care that he lies;
they just hate the stories.)

Fred's photos showing rustic charm,
more than we saw, are larger lies.

My shed in mind is unwanted now,
memories as painful as splinters,
but too deep to pull.

"Toys not put away are lost," Mother said.
She loved it when we took things to the shed.

COMMON CARRIER OF CHOICE

Dressed in formal gray
regardless of occasion

sidewalks

never talk strike
never leave before we're ready.

Panhandlers
backbreaking cracks
a patch of ice

hardly rank as terrors.

Sidewalks are so quiet

we swallow one
after another

quickly losing count.

FAMILY RESEMBLANCE

Never blame the other driver.
Adjust the drapes, not the thermostat.
Do crosswords in ink.
Penmanship counts.

My sister Carol
influenced me the most,
not what I expected,
nor she.

Carol was a given
in the background,
hardly noticed,
let alone followed.

Carol was
a thousand little inflexibilities.

Living with Carol meant
connecting all the dots
not just finishing a picture.

HIGH SCHOOL

GRAVEYARD SHIFT

Recruiters work the streets
looking for idle youths ready to dig.

Some refuse no matter how high the pay,
but most are eager and figure
if the dead don't dicker
neither should they.

Since the earth is in motion and caskets travel
backhoes are no good in the older sections
where there are no vaults. Shovels must be used.

I like best when you first get deep enough
that your head is below ground level
and the loose dirt is flying out with a geyser effect.

The biggest pain is remembering where you put the sod
and hanging around until everyone leaves
before you dare throw any dirt back.

MAGNITUDE 9.2: A SITKA SUMMER

The great
(a technical term for quakes over 8.0 on the Richter Scale)
Alaskan earthquake of 1964 was the largest
earthquake in North America
and the second largest ever recorded
(largest occurred in Chile in 1960),
but there is no need to worry about rain in Sitka:
it rains every day.

Airplane tickets are inscribed with a mantra:
this plane may never take off,
if it does take off it may not fly where you want to go,
and when it puts down,
if it puts down,
you may be further from your destination
than when you took off.
We are not responsible
for Acts of God.

The summer of '64 I was not responsible
but I was keen on
Acts of God.
In Alaska everything burned,
for example, and when I arrived
my host was still shaking from the tsunami
and a recent backyard mauling.

I resented the babysitter's loud and foolish
love-making with her boyfriend
in the basement, so I took revenge
by hiding her clothes. Trouble was,
she had plenty of extra clothes.
Rain was no problem: it rains every day.

During one of our rare reconciliations,
the sitter asked me to set a fire.
I said there was no fire wood.
She told me to use her employer's (my host's)
collection of Indian carvings.
How was I to know the ones that looked
the worst were worth the most?

We lived on an island. I had no car.
My host refused to offer me a ride
since his car was for official business only.
He advised if I fell ill I'd better
not go to the hospital on our island
since only Indians were admitted.
My interest in the Acts of God fell short
in getting me admitted to St. Michael's Orthodox Cathedral.
My opening bid was for them to conduct the service
in English since my Russian was rusty.
My host did not like me because I favored
Barry Goldwater for president.
I liked to wander among the bunkers built to protect
Sitka from a Japanese invasion
but now used as tombs for TB patients.

My best idea came to me the day we
visited an Alaskan pioneer who lived
in a large and magnificent log cabin
with a wall of glass overlooking the bay.

Two years after my visit, Sitka burned,
taking down St. Michael's, just like everything burns in
Alaska.
Just like it rains every day.

COLLEGE

THE HAIRY LOLLIPOP

The juice of fresh fruit

dribbles down

and makes my whiskers sticky.

WHAT THE LECTURER SAID

The lecturer said King was dead.
None of us knew,
we had been at dinner,
discussing what we expected
the speaker to say.

None of us knew Jacques Derrida
would write his "Ends of Man" essay
in the interval between
King's death and the invasion
of the universities of Paris.
Or that Derrida would date his essay
as begun on the day of King's death.

The lecturer said King came to nonviolence
from Henry Thoreau by way of Gandhi.
The lecturer said that was a good way to come in.

The lecturer asked us who we thought
would take King's place.
None of us knew.
The lecturer asked us who
were the great living men and women
of prophetic imagination in our lives.
None of us knew.
The lecturer was sad.

The lecturer said at any given time
one should have at least 100 unsung prophets
as colleagues in the struggle.

The lecturer sat down and drank from a thermos.
Someone said, "Sir, can you go on?"
The lecturer stood up and said,
"Bear with me, please".
Then the lecturer turned his back on us
and wrote on the board.
He made a chart, a family tree sort of chart,
a very simple chart, and we all copied it.

Later when we talked about the lecture
none of us knew what to do.
None of us knew what to think.
We compared notes, we agreed
on what the lecturer said.

We all agreed the lecturer was clear.
We did not know what to think.

The lecturer said that Jesus and Socrates met
on the way to heaven.
He said they both thought highly of Plato and expected great
things of him.

(Only later did we learn that the day before he died,
King said, in a sermon in the Masonic temple of Memphis,
"I would see Plato, Aristotle, Socrates, Euripides and
Aristophanes as they discussed the great and eternal
issues of reality.")

The lecturer said Socrates and Jesus talked
of practical matters, crowd control, their doubts.
Jesus said he urged mercy for his killers,
they killed in ignorance.
Socrates asked Jesus if the crucifixion
would save him, ex post facto.
Jesus said he did not know.
Then Jesus smirked.
Jesus asked Socrates why he did not escape
when he had a chance.
Socrates smirked and said it was clear
Jesus had not read Plato's Crito.
Jesus smirked.
Then Jesus said something
that was hard to understand,
so the lecturer skipped that part.

The lecturer drank more from the thermos.

The lecturer said we should read Marcus Aurelius.
The lecturer said we must learn to read
even when there is no time to read.
Even when we are caught up in the struggle,
even when we are out of hope.
Then the lecturer said
we must learn to see
when there is no light.
We need to navigate our own way, he said.
The lecturer said we had to play our part,
that this was the teaching of the Gita
as Gandhi knew.

Then we heard the drum beat.
The lecturer said that was the sound
of a different drummer.
We were puzzled,
but we did hear the beat.

We wondered what the lecturer
had in his thermos.
The lecturer was a guest lecturer,
introduced as Mr. Valiant-for-Truth.
We had no idea if he was for real.
He had a sword and a shield.
He also had marks and scars.
He began the lecture saying
"Martin Luther King, Jr., is dead."
He asked us who would get Martin's
sword and shield of nonviolence.
He said Martin would carry
his marks and scars with him
as a witness, just as Mr. Valiant-for-Truth
carried his own marks and scars
when he went to his reward.
Martin's sword and shield, he said,
would go to whomever could get them.
So of course at first we thought
this was just some crazy drunk.

We listen to everyone,
my friends and I.
We enjoy all sorts of lectures.
We have dinner before and speculate
on what the lecturer might say.
Then we go out afterwards and discuss the lecture
and talk about what we will do in light of the lecture. Best of
all, we like lectures that change our lives. Lectures that set
us on a different course.

Socrates would go all night, talking, drinking.
King was a pastor caught up in the civil rights struggle but
rarely missing Sunday morning at Ebenezer.

The lecturer said we had to dig deeper into the roots of non-
violence, of conscience and of action.

The lecturer said we had to go back to Thoreau's education in
moral philosophy at Harvard,
and his reading of Butler on conscience.

The lecturer said
we had to understand how Thoreau could absorb Butler
and understand why Gandhi rejected Butler
when the Quakers tried to force Butler on him.

The lecturer said we had to see
our own patterns of attraction and repulsion

The lecturer said we should read Emerson.

The lecturer said we needed to carry a copy
of Emerson at all times, as Nietzsche did.

The lecturer said we would never understand
Emerson's reading of Butler; it was too deep.

The lecturer said
that what we know
is but a point
compared to what
we do not know.

The lecturer said we have no idea what is going on
yet conscience remains as the candle of the Lord within us.

The lecturer said Emerson was
just Butler's assistant,
a butler to Butler;
that Emerson was still a huge inspiration
to Dewey and many others,
that those others included Cornel West.

We understood some of this,
but none of us had heard of Cornel West.
West at that time was in high school, unpublished,
but active in organizing for civil rights,
demanding courses in black studies.
West seemed to know
what to think and what to do.

A few of us knew Ginsberg
cut the lines on Butler's Analogy
from Howl, and we knew our Dewey,
but we did not know Dewey was so down on Butler,
just the way Gandhi was down on Butler
and for the same reason:
because old-school types
had tried to force
the Butler on them.

We talked and thought
but we did not know
what to say
or what to think.

We talked and talked without knowing what to say.
Mr. Valiant-for-Truth was clear, we agreed,
only many years later did we come to know
Mr. Valiant-for-Truth was talking to us.

We had read the words of Butler about redemption,
that it does not matter what your theory of redemption is,
what matters is that you feel you are redeemed,
believe you are redeemed,
and even that does not matter
as long as you live as one who is redeemed.

Years later we were still puzzled
by what the lecturer said,
years later we found out
who Dr. Cornel West was.
Years later we read West,
we heard him lecture.
We heard Cornel West talk of Socrates.
Talk of Emerson.
Talk of Dewey.
Talk of King.
We heard. We discussed.

We understood (somewhat).
We agreed.

But we still could not translate
our talk into action.

Socrates drank his hemlock.
King took his bullet.
Emerson lost his job.
Thoreau spent his night in jail.
Gandhi was in jail all the time,
until he was killed.
Dewey faced relentless criticism.
Butler died just when he was finally
going to be able to do
what he most wanted
and be of most help.
Yet the day before Dr. King died,
he told the assembly in the Masonic Temple of Memphis
that it did not matter if he died,
that he was ready to pass on. He was 39.

They all live. For all I know
they were there that night long ago
when Mr. Valiant for Truth lectured
and told us Martin Luther King, Jr.,
had been shot.

The royal line is broken.
The lineage just a construct.

These days I'm thinking less about who speaks for me
and more about who speaks to me.
More about what is left for me to do
and less about how I will die.

Nothing works.

Nothing is more an insult to Dr. King
than to celebrate his birthday without
living in the spirit,
without redemption and amendment of life,
without conversion, without dedication.

True remembrance of Dr. King
is in recognition of the signs of our terrible times
and to bear the weight of this sad time.
The dead refuse to bury their dead

King and West and Butler
and Thoreau and Emerson and Gandhi
live in our heads.

We must read them
even when there is no time to read,
even when we do not understand,
even when we lack courage.
This is what the lecturer said April 4, 1968,
and this is what I think we should do now.

Derrida's essay on "The Ends of Man,"
The essay begun at the time of King's death,
The essay Derrida dated as begun
at the time of King's death,
was a success and was published
in Buffalo, New York,
September, 1969.

THE DILDO

Many years ago (I'm 61 now)
visiting a woman I barely knew
when suddenly she said, "Excuse me
but I feel the need to masturbate,
would you be a sweet and pick me up
an extra-large dildo that vibrates?"

Maintaining appearances I sped to "Show Time XXX"
and bought a good size gaudy fleshy hard dildo
from the medium price rack.

I was pleased that she was pleased,
but before she could pleasure herself
full tilt another funny thing happened.

This woman I barely knew emerged
from her bedroom in a robe holding
the Dildo and complaining, "I do not
know how to insert the batteries."
"That so," I dead panned showing her how.

Years later,
a man I never knew
a man who nearly died,
asked me to replace his fan
during a heat wave,
which I did
at the risk
of my job.

PISSING IN GOOD COMPANY

Note to the reader: the poet is male but is writing as a female.

Sleepy Hollow Cemetery opens at 7 in the morning,
so I arrived before 5 intent on some contemplation
prolonged and private, a plan of some merit but less
well executed since by the time I'd found Emerson's
grave on Authors Ridge my bladder was ready to burst,
not at all embarrassed if I knew its distress
to the extent I was ready to piss in my pants and get
it over with, still determination can work wonders
of invention, so I dropped my pants and squatted next
to the marker, so if apprehended at all I would appear
to be engaged in nothing more offensive than some
unauthorized grave-tending, then in another burst
of the creative as would make Ralph smile, I did
a slow release despite my pain and urgency with
each drop grateful I am woman and get to piss like
a girl with none of the crude male competitiveness
of who can arc farther, no, for me as for Ralph Waldo
the question is rather how deep one goes, my thin
yellow cord going deep indeed reaching my man
and quenching his long thirst for the non-conformity
one needs to be a man. With each timed release I
sent the sage a terse and personal message of gratitude,
complaint, perplexity, irreverence. No, I say to my
Ralph, as he receives my urine, my sacred fluid,
a part of myself I cannot part with without ceremony,
a ceremony worthy of being heard of by others in need,
if not all over the world. They did not beat a path to me
that morning I pissed on Emerson's grave, but so what
if they had? It was a good piss, I, and perhaps you,
shall remember it fondly whenever, for the rest of my life,

I relieve myself and remember to take the time to think of what matters most, how the waste I no longer can use goes back into the great moral economy that brought Emerson to Concord, to me, and I to him, this early, dark, morning, still dark, still cold as I pull up my pants preparing to make my escape, my day's work done before breakfast, a broad margin of life spread before me.

GRAD SCHOOL

GO WEST

It's not easy
to leave Concord,
partly because it's such
a pretty place but also because
the traffic is terrible. Should you manage
to depart in good spirits, go west to Northampton for
        Edwards
then north to Burlington for the Dewey birthplace. Now turn
        around,
and go down to Albany. In just a few hours you will be at
        Teachers' College
where you will find little besides a plaque and an attitude of
        excellence in inquiry
to remind you of John Dewey and William Heard Kilpatrick.
No matter.
Press on to Princeton, where you can have tea with Cornel
        West,
before heading back upstate this time taking 17 to
        Binghamton
then 81 to Syracuse, to grab a quick one in Fayetteville with
Matilda Joslyn Gage, or perhaps her impersonator, how
they love to fool the unwary. I want to get you high
so you will stay high and so it will be safe to
drive to Chicago in the dark, because
the ghost of John Dewey never did
figure out how to leave that place.

Note: Cornell University is the westernmost of the Ivy League
universities.

ITHACA AND ITS POSSIBILITIES (1963)

Everyone wears turtlenecks
at Rochester's Spent Club,
except one woman, older, relaxed,
so I least expected her responding
first and loudest just as I finished
—up from her seat she bounded
down to the stage's edge and shouted:

You must, you must, you must see
the gorges of Ithaca,
you must see them tonight.
It's clear from your work
the gorges will do good,
so go go go right now.

What's the matter? Need money?
Here, she said, no forget money;
you don't need money,
car, do you have a car, no car?
All right, take my car.

As if we rehearsed the move
her arm was straight out and up
like saluting some Nazi,
she offered a bunch of keys
as big as a small hedgehog.

Not wanting to obey this mad woman
and not wanting to go in a stranger's car
in the middle of the night
to a strange place I had no particular purpose to visit
but wanting far less to have to deal with her
in any other way, I went off:

Who could foresee the glory
and the tomfoolery
that lay ahead?
It's 96 all the way, she said,
when I took her keys:
fear, curiosity, gratitude, anxiety:
the good stress
that is the key to longevity,

Later.
That's it, we're done:
I must go to see the gorges,
the gorges will do me good.

Don't ask me how the prophet knew.

This much I've learned tonight:
it takes a hard poem to bring Ulysses home.

A MEMO FROM THE COMMISSIONER OF EDUCATION

One day Johnny's teacher told the class
to go home and write a poem
about the nameless, nonviolent power
from which all things originate
and to which all return.

Johnny took the teacher literally,
and as usual finished his homework
in plenty of time to shoot
a few baskets before dinner.

Other pupils expressed themselves
in the form of a three-act play,
which they performed
for the class.

One kid brought in a picture of a koala
she had carelessly torn
from someone's
magazine.

The teacher said
that was OK.

RÉSUMÉ

After I quit my day job,
I worked comedy clubs throughout the Northwest
and visited Mars twice.

I was imprisoned for writing bad checks
and released for good behavior.

I subscribe to a well-known magazine,
I've been interviewed for a public opinion poll.
I've been called a liar and a braggart,
last year I was invited to join the National Geographic Society

My best literary work was lost in a fire three years ago,
my spirit has never flagged.

Friends often admire my clothes,
some people still lend me money.

When my style of humor went out of fashion,
I spent ten years perfecting a valve
that made travel to Mars easier.

For me, making money has been less of a concern
than making a statement.

The reason I left Mars was trouble with the language.

NIGERIA

ANT INFESTATION

Ant infestation begins with just a few in the kitchen
—not a problem—
 easy to think you've got such the advantage
they could never be more than a nuisance
then once it gets to be every day
you just get tired of the killing
and let them live
what harm can they do?

Not much perhaps until they appear
in cups and on plates not just near the garbage

you can try to interrupt their supply line
let them live as long as they don't bite

or don't bite much
or don't bite all the time

for example, once the infestation gets going
all you have to do
is leave a little bit
of soap on an undershirt
and if you put it on
without looking
they will be all over you
but probably more afraid of you
than you of them.

So you learn to live with them
and they with you
some people are put off by ants all over
but that's their prejudice
that's what they have to live with.

ON THE WAY TO BAR BEACH

The conductor spoke with such an accent
I could hardly understand anything.

The conductor was
enthusiasm undiminished
by my incomprehension,
an animation more appropriate
for art or religion
than mundane directions,
affable patience
in the face
of ineffable ignorance,
while we were never so awkwardly misplaced.

The most commonplace
familiar to them
an impenetrable nebula to us,
yet above the honkers
anxious to be on their way,
the conductor's voice
was clear and strong,

reassuring not just that we
would find Bar Beach,
but that finding it our effort
(and their sacrifice)
would be rewarded
over and over.

Note: Bar Beach is a place of execution in Lagos, Nigeria.

MARRIAGE
AND HOUSEHOLD

PRESENT AND ACCOUNTED FOR

Birds dart.
        Linda looks.
                We relax.

Clouds cover
        the hills, the fields, the houses.
                Clouds cover, Linda prepares.

Linda's patience rests,
        ready at roadside,
                watching.

Underfoot,
        below leaves
                and grass,

silent creatures
        mind their own business.
                The sunlight is not

for them now.
        It warms
                the field above.

SMALL BUT SELECT

Watch your step
going through
the Japanese
garden.

Take the small path
on your left
down to where
the greenhouse
used to be.

Last summer
we restored
the greenhouse
as a good-sized,
sun-lit reading
room,

but the book-storage
areas are sun-free
and climate
controlled.

Everything is where
you'd expect
in a small
but select
library.

GOING TOO FAR

I write, therefore I am.
I am, therefore I write.

On the way to work
I dropped a comma
and when I bent to pick it up
I slit my trousers
so I had to stand all day
at work with my legs
tight together
to keep warm;
still things worked out:

I got a better view of what
everyone else did at work:
not much, really, but fun
to watch on a day when
you have a hole in your pants.
Keep writing, keep revising,
and keep in touch (with me).

I find that if I do NOT trim the wick
of my love-light then I get a softer
glow and drop more commas,
which is a good thing. No.
Your right; I'm sure it's your right;
it's too early in the day for it to be my right,
anyway. Whatever. Want to appear younger
than you are? (Of course you do.)
Say "whatever" instead of "works for me,"
but stay alert for sudden changes in fashion.

MARRIAGE MANUAL

The first time my wife torched our bedroom,
I was hanging a picture downstairs.

I ran to the street in pajamas,
I should have seen trouble ahead.

The fire marshal's not a bad therapist;
he has to finish before we can go in.

The children chat with the neighbors,
newspapers get us all wrong.
Perhaps it was something I said.

This time I've eaten too many Red Cross doughnuts,
I just want to get warm in my bed.

She's not to blame.
Midnight picture hanging is noisy,
bad dancing makes life hell.

OWED TO SIMPLICITY

down-size consumption for relaxed fit
take care not to over-load, maintain
the end-in-view whilst tunefully
expounding how to live more
with less and less. Three
local wines and a coin
of endangered breed
orphans now home
for the holidays.

CANDLE POWER

When we ran out of candles,
dinner was delayed half an hour
while I went to get some.

Now a mindless compulsion,
candles were once the only light,

and family life was sound by nature,
      so now with artificial light
      we need an art to make things right.

Mother used to say:
      The bell calls us to dinner;
      the candle keeps all else out,
      and the habit was formed without argument.

After years of annoyance, lost matches,
fast-drip wax and just too much stuff on the table,
with children of my own and feeling the tug
of concentric rings of enticement,
only now do I see the light and feel the heat

and the magnetism of the candle,
the little light that gives us, briefly,
a larger darkness to enjoy.

DENNY'S DAY

Sometimes you wake up and you know it's a Denny's day.
You wake up thinking about the bacon and eggs scramble
and the thick toast thick with butter and you just want to
get the wife and kids into the car and get to Denny's
and start the day by having a really good time.

So you do, and everything is swell, and the waitress
is cute and smiling and neatly dressed, early in the morning,
and the kids are quiet for once while she reviews the menu
with everyone, and then she says Denny is having a special
promotion and if you order two kids' breakfasts you
get a free Denny coloring-book and with two adult
breakfasts you get a free blow-job for dad, and your
wife says, "Oh, honey, a blow job, isn't that the
thing you always said you wanted? This must
be your lucky day."

So you go out back where they give the blow-jobs,
only it isn't the perky cute waitress, it's an older woman,
but still attractive and good at what she does,
and the line is long, but you wait, chatting with
the guys, and sure enough you make it back
to the table just when the waitress is bringing
your breakfasts, and everyone gets the
right order and everyone is happy
and it's the start of a happy day,
a happy Denny's day.

RIGHT OUT OF PLACE

My son kept asking me about the man
reading Mailer's Naked, while Andre
decked himself in terror at Jake's snake.
"You'll understand when you're older,"
I lied, playing for time.

An outrageously normal man
reading about time machines
and existentially futile combat.

Years from now the boy will know
to squeeze off "I find that odd"
only when he has stopped breathing
and is dead sure of his target.

Years from now,
he'll know how curiosity kills.

MY NICK

I'm sorry, Nick's not here,
he's bought a house without a landline

so when he feels he must,
he goes there, turns off his cell.

There's no way for you to reach him,
no way for me to reach him, with my bitterness.

He's still my lover fulltime, but he needs his own time,
away from everyone, away even from me.

"We're not married," he said when I complained.
"The Nick who is your lover is the same Nick,

the same lover, even when, especially when,
he's out of touch, at his own place, on his own time."

We kiss. He explains some more,
gently, lovingly, persuasively.

Hurt and confused as I am, I don't feel right,
bothering you with my Nick.

SPIRITUALITY

INVOCATION

I saw six men talking to a girl with bad eyesight.
I saw six men gawking at a girl who would not leave.

I saw six men talking to a girl just trying to read.
I saw six men talking, talking in harmony.

I saw six men wave, saw them wave so the girl could see.
I saw time run short and hold that girl,

hold her so she could not leave.
I saw six men talking, talking tough,

talking in harmony.
I saw six men with their ties tied just so.

I saw the light and I saw the light surrender,
surrender to men talking, talking in harmony.

ABRAHAM

What were you thinking
Snug in your tent,
You patriarch you?

You with your private army.
Is it an offense to faith if I research you?
Look under your tent?

I guess you don't need a fan club when you are the father of
a   great nation.

What, Father Abraham, do you think of the Jews?
What did you think when you first heard God speak?
Can you even remember the details of the Bible stories?
Or are they nothing but folklore?

Do many people pray to you, Father Abraham, or is it just
        me?

What were you thinking, Father Abraham,
when you argued Sodom and Gomorrah with God,
what were you thinking?
No one ever argued with God before.

Still, you got your great nation.
Sodom and Gomorrah,
whatever the exact number of righteous people, got
        annihilated
only to rise again in trashy fundamentalist tracts
and as a singing group in "Tuscaloosa's Calling Me,"
a Broadway musical whose title tune grabbed me so
much when I first heard it on the car radio
that I did not return home until I had bought
        the album.

TESTIMONY OF THE WITNESSES

Church work educational, cultural, artistic scholarly
aims at a refinement of the vision, aims at a Christian life.
Whatever the source the vision, is un-constant,
blurring, its object distorted, we are led astray.

Dante, Bunyan, Milton and Melville
have constancy to be rediscovered,
as do the great Biblical narratives
—especially prophetic and apocalyptic material—
and the pre-biblical stories—the Epic of Gilgamesh.

The great Anglican poets down to Geoffrey Hill,
existential drama Gabriel Marcel
and especially Godot and all the works of Dante's admirer
Mr. Beckett:

"the vision here is of two monkeys in a miserable cage,
clinging desperately to one another with a sort of
        infinite distress."
Even with this heritage, it remains difficult to see the vision in
more recent material, today's material, our material
hard to grasp what is right before us.

but surely the mission of the church in the contemporary
        world
cannot be merely to rehash "the classics",
(prophets don't recite other prophets)
but to incite every member to vision,
to see and be seen in one's chosen medium,
to underwrite, materially and spiritually, all forms of creative
        action,

to collect, display and illuminate the most recent art, liturgi-
cal crafts, music, graphics, words written and spoken, actions
and organizations with social and ethical significance,

to deliver to the congregation in intelligible form:
the end-products of Church of England history,
of Christian history,
of human history,
of the whole history
of life on earth,

to show the continuity and unity of theological speculation
to make every member part of the story an active discussant,

to see all public prayers and sermons as art forms,
all art forms as public prayers,
sermons that pray, prayers that preach.

To conceive that which cannot be conceived,
as St. Anselm did,
To say that which cannot be said
by coming to terms with the failure of words

Poems are not superior products
by which we go the creator one better,
they are more like a bodily discharge
indicative of inner healing.

The success of a poem or of any form of mystical expression
is not that it does justice to its object
but that it does not pretend to be more or better than it is.

Its falsehood, distortion, even its offense certifies its
          legitimacy.

Worthwhile poems are never appropriate.
Worthwhile poems distract us from our fondest distractions

Writing poetry is the counter-weight to other types of writing.

Embedded clichés
work havoc
by impersonating
the deft touch
the slight scent
the end.

BELIEF AND PRACTICE

Once God died
the angels were pressed to find work.

Most are dead or retired now;
only Gabriel and Michael
are on all-night call.
It amazes Gabe how people complain
about his soiled robe and tarnished halo.

Ingratitude is eternal.
The cumulative effects of petty thefts
have been driving angels
out of business,
out of existence.

"Miracle" is stolen
wherever it isn't nailed down.

IN THE FORM OF A PRAYER

My issue with Madonna is
that, yes, like a prayer
but not merely like a prayer is a prayer
but totally agreeing with Bill Clinton
that what that means all depends on what the meaning of is
is,
so I say let us say
in the form of a prayer,
what is in the form of a prayer is a prayer
(and what the is means there is that the writing is informed
by prayer)

and what is in the form of a prayer may be like a prayer

or not so much like any prayer we've heard before.

so to conclude now right before the AMEN,
I'd say listen to see if you have heard this prayer before

listen to see if this is like a prayer
listen for the form of the prayer

see if it works for you
know that to work is to pray and to pray is to work, AMEN.

DAMAGED GOODS

You
   soiled
      unkept
         drooling
            wheezing
               self-absorbed
                  failed
                     tedious
                        pestering
                           childlike
                             dependent
       INMATES

having little
   prospect of ever
      being free
         to walk the streets,
            you know
               freedom is
                  a whole lot more
                     than nothing
                        left to lose

       AND YET

without your dementia
        my patience would not be tried
            my kindness would not be showered
                there's not one in 500,000 could
                    care for you as I do
                        the world's not perfect
                            but it's
                                admirably
                                arranged

TRAVEL

GRAND PRIX, VEGAS AND THE DELTA CONNECTION

We are on the ground at JFK
delayed by a door that refuses to close.
After 7 pm sorties to Europe
push the pull back and taxi to at least an hour.

There are only a handful of us on the tiny
Delta Connection. The man behind me is
going to Rochester to be an attendant
on a flight from Rochester to L.A. via Memphis.

The only passenger on his FedEx cargo flight
is a horse, a horse with a $10,000 ticket.
Every day, the man says, thousands of horses
fly all over the world for races and shows.

We are on the ground so long I have time to ponder
how romantic "The Delta Connection" sounds.
The man says he was in Egypt, a delta to write home about,
last week and had a few days in Arabia before that.

"Delta Connection," very romantic.
The man carries a case of tranquilizers
but is reluctant to use them since horses with drugs
can't race and don't show well.

We have been on the tarmac a long time,
so our attendant says we can have all the free
alcohol we want. We don't have to worry
about racing or showing well.

The man is only going as far as L.A. but he is certain,
he says, the horse is bound for the Grand Prix, Las Vegas.
Delta Connection is not romantic, Delta Connection is scary
as if we were in a dark marsh dabbling in the occult.

Someone asks the man how he got into the horse
transport business. "My father escorted horses," he says,
which begs the question. I want to ask how his father
got started, but I am too shy.

The man says, "on a transport plane
I can sit in the cockpit if I want."
I try to imagine a horse named "Delta Connection"
in the cockpit, but I am unsuccessful.

As we are about to land in Rochester,
I think about the parade clowns who sweep
up after the horses in the line of march,
and I wonder if, by chance, I will ever meet

the person who dreamed up the phrase
"Delta Connection". If I do, I won't be
too shy to ask whether "Delta Connection"
was intended to be romantic.

I still can't imagine a horse in the cockpit.
I can't imagine what it would be like to be a horse
in the Grand Prix, Vegas. I can't imagine
what it would be like to be a horse in Egypt or Arabia.

I can only imagine what it would be
like to have clowns
following me in a parade.
Maybe that is the Delta Connection.

THOUGHTS EN ROUTE TO A PRESENTATION

The watchman enjoys his work. So does
      the accomplished seamstress.
Yesterday the gated garden was unlocked. No time
      to linger.
Agreed: One thought at a time is enough
      —without distraction.
Thanks for the note. Was it———perhaps———
      For someone else?
The center is still. But where
      is the center?
The kitchen needs cleaning. So the frogs seem
      to say.
Leaves stop falling And let the snow fall
      without objection.
This line of eleven makes up for
      the line of nine.
This small basket took three years to weave
      for you.

STAYING PUT

Six years ago the four of us
moved to Montana to get away
from the city riots
and face our own problems.

Without the shield of distraction
reality pressed in so hard
it damn near crushed the children.

Driving back to Detroit
we stop—somewhere—just for aspirin.

As we stare at hundreds of pain killers
basking in fluorescence,
the sound of casual talk
overheard at the counter screams
stay put.

POETRY
AND PHILOSOPHY

SOCRATES TIME

Socrates treks by night
through the unseen streets
unhampered by darkness
carrying home his thoughts
of other things,
things most men never dream,
things left unsaid
in casual conversation,
thoughts dark, wet,
hard to hold for long,
thoughts poisonous, perhaps,
best kept under wraps,
to be shown only to a few
pals huddled in a dark
corner of Athens,
guys who savor rare thoughts,
guys willing to go the distance
up to a point
then to settle down
to sleep while Socrates
makes his way home
to shower, shave
(perhaps, a little)
and prepare himself
for another day
in another world.

ONLY A SECOND TO LOSE

Here is what Mary Ann did one day.
She went out into the woods,
to an old well she knew about.
Very deep with muck at the bottom
and filled with insects.
She took off all her clothes
and jumped into the well
with the express intent
that she would suffer
as much as possible
before she died.

We pride ourselves on "knowing"
that Mary Ann must have had a mental
problem because we think no person
with a "right mind" (our expression) would
willingly go to a slow and painful death.

Perhaps, but consider this, suppose we
were all issued pills when we turned twenty-one,
pills which if swallowed would cause a swift
and painless death, and suppose it became
common for people to swallow these pills
whenever they became blue or discouraged
with life and felt they had little or nothing to lose.

In such a society, might it not become
fashionable to do oneself in more dramatically,
and might not those who resented and disliked
their bodies, their lives or themselves,
for whatever reason, soundly conclude
that the best way to do something
would be to skip the easy way
out and distinguish at least
the end of life by making
it slow and painful?

COME AND GO: A MATHEMATICAL PROPOSITION

Mr. Bertrand Russell sat
at his hard, brown, desk
working a proposition of mathematics.

She watched.
"So, Mr. Bertrand Russell, show me
your mathematical proposition.
No, really, I adore maths, Mr. Bertrand Russell."
[She is naked now.]

Russell is hard,
hard as the brown table,
hard as mathematics.

"Show me the proposition
[silence],
I want to see your mathematical proposition,
Mr. Russell."
[Russell removes his trousers.]

"Don't be hard with me, Mr. Russell,
tell me about your mathematical proposition.
Tell me about it.
Then we can fuck all you want."
[Her legs spread wide. Russell speechless.]

"Oh, God," Russell says to himself,
what am I getting into?"
"God" Russell keeps saying
as her hand works his erection.
"Not yet, not yet,
first tell me about the proposition,
the mathematical proposition."
Russell enters without effort.
"They are all different;
every one is different,"
Russell thinks.
She is silent.
Silent as a mathematician hard at work.

Russell comes,
too soon.
There is no fuck.

"Fucking is hard,"
Russell says to himself,
"as hard as mathematics,
as hard as my table. And,"
Russell goes on to himself
(not daring to say it),
"there are no words. Words fail."

"So, Mr. Bertrand, here is your pipe,
          may I fill it?
                    may I light it?"

Russell, naked, is silent
Russell, no longer hard, is silent.
But she, still not satisfied, speaks.

She is firm, knowing whereof she speaks:

"The Pythagorean Plato advised,"
she tells him,
           "that by the use of problems,
as in geometry,
                      we let the things of heaven
come
and go. Come, and go."

WAR & POLITICS

WARTIME SERENADE

Hot war, cold war no war
at all. Holy war, profane war
peace war for fun and game war
Moslems feel offended by sexy songs
we hold dear, so violence flares unneeded
when we seem insensitive to their inhibition.
Muslims must learn to deal with sex,
we must learn to deal with them
and all of us regardless of
religion must play the
hand we're dealt.

The reason
torture works is
it puts the mind
under such stress
it is impossible to lie.
Under torture the body
uses all its energy to survive,
there is none left to fuel a lie.
When you are mad
mad angry not mad crazy
emotion is too high to think.

WHAT IF PACIFIST PIRATES RULED THE WORLD?

A Treasure Chest of Poems for World Domination
No Map Required: Parrots Optional
Profanity Prohibited: Compliance Minimal

We now know it was 1884 when implantation began.
Implantation is the entry of Artificial Control into a system.
Previously the will of God controlled the unfolding of events.
With God out of the picture human ingenuity had its turn.

The human condition leaves a lot to be desired.
No one sober thinks all is for the best in this best of all
          possible worlds.
Believers think God can fix things;
humanists think we can kiss and make it better

The pacifist pirates who rule the world turn to drugs as the
sensible alternative.

"Why don't we just steal a boat load of drugs
          the ingestion of which will make everyone
          honestly believe all is for the best
          in this the best of all possible worlds?"

Seeing there are no objections, the chair sets the plan in
          motion.
We don the traditional skull and crossbones bibs and grab
some reading material knowing there might be a long wait
for   the right ship.

(If I weren't a pirate,
I would definitely be a surrealist,
so I strap the History of Surrealism to my back.)

With a hearty "Hi-Ho-Long-John-Silver-Away"
We set sail, and far sooner than expected spy
a rich galleon of pharmaceuticals.
The crew is unarmed and underpaid,
so persuading them to join our merry crew is a snap.

As the sun sets we join hands in the dance of universal inebriation,
We hop like Lindy, trot like a fox and even get in a stroll with a twist.
In the future this is how children will be taught to live,
With songs, with stories, with substances.

A DAY AT THE ANARCHIST BOOK FAIR

What's this? Ungoverned. Ungovernable.

Oft time not law-abiding.

Some seem settled in.
        Some just passing through.
                Some drinking beer.
                        None inspiring confidence.

An anarchist fair isn't billed
as a school of etiquette,
but if we're going to improve our image,
we've got to improve our image

Or we'll be bowling alone in the anarchist league.

DEATH BY INSTITUTION

Were we to Educate,
it would be by Engrossment
to Church with Awe——and shock
at the cruel acts of the Gods
and Politic as a man among
men and women, willing to discard
their old sovereignty
as willingly as some nudist
disrobes only to take on
a new outer wear of skin and hair,
with a body of language of your own,

not some cat who wants to be let in
to find his mat, his mate, his mandolin
or whatever has taken his soul by storm
this hour of this day and not some other
time less ferocious, less real, gentle,
perhaps, but vapid, as I long to be done
with this institution, with all institutions,
long for the day when fewer spiders crawl
the walls, fewer silverfish live in
and there are not so many lizards in the basement
I have trouble getting to the canned goods,
all these being graphics intended to show

how I wish I could show them the moon.

PITCH FOR PEACE

I rise to make a pitch for peace,
friends, Romans, and hecklers.
I rise without a poem to read,
but with an agenda:
to plead for integration
of anti-war elements,
for recognition that
those who fight and those who
fund the fighting are neither
more evil nor ignorant than we,
but mired in the misapprehension
that violence works,
that violence wins,
that poetry does not work.

When a warrior or would-be warrior
hears a disarming poem,
seeds of doubt are planted;
every time one or two of us
leverages assets for peace,
the field is prepared.
Raising poetic consciousness
in farmers' markets, on downtown streets,
in places of worship, at shopping malls,
visiting private clubs on or off campus
or on used car lots,
we are in pitched battle for peace.

Our sorry collective consciousness
needs deep cleaning,
deeper reading of Thoreau, Gandhi and King,
greater willingness to take one's chances
on the field of peace
even while the military-industrial complex
is whining with its demands.

I yield the balance of my time to the war dead,
the widows and orphans, to prisoners,
and to those whose lives were irreparably
disrupted by governments who kill.

LINES COMPOSED AT COURSE REGISTRATION

"I hear Intro to Freud is a gut.
You can sleep through it as long
as you dream and tell; you can
bitch all you want. A girl got an
'A' for the course just because she
went hysterical when she failed
the final exam; when this guy BSed
his way through an essay the teacher
said it was the freest association he
had ever seen and should be published."

"The catch is you have to buy a couch
of your own from the prof for two grand;
one has to eat, he keeps saying; also
if you care about the sex jokes you have
to know Latin. I heard one guy got
an 'F' and was sure it was a slip but the
prof said sometimes an 'F' is just an 'F'."

"I know for a fact this guy killed his dad
and fucked his mother right before going
to study-group and they made him a teaching
assistant. When I took it, this kid showed me
his dick when the lecture got boring and it
was so cute I wished I had one too. Then
the teacher started talking about me in front
of everyone and I turned beet red. The class
is weird, but like I say, it's a gut, and my GPA
is really hurting."

DEPARTURE

ALEXANDRA

I've written fine lines
with Alexandra my muse.

She comes in the morning
and deftly sets down.

I've given her gifts,
but she will not wait:
Sometimes I think
she is seeing someone else.

Middle of last summer
I gave my muse all I had:

Gave her my house.
Gave her my wife.
Gave her my little kids, too.

Gave her my job,
and gave her my dandruff,
which would not stay anyway.

Alexandra stayed my hand
when I offended;
she tied my tongue dry and tight.

My muse, she kids, she jokes,
like the milkman of my youth.

We've talked and touched,
so I know she is real.
Gods, demons, angels,
heroes and tides:

They all seem real to me.
All seem real to me.

ALEX

Alexandra, my muse showed up this afternoon,
unusual, she's usually a morning muse.

Alexandra came to me naked,
something I thought I'd never see,
but stranger still she went to my closet
and dressed in my clothes.

I tried not to look while Alexandra went through my room,
went through the whole house,
taking small things of value,
breaking legs on the furniture,
tearing and staining the upholstered pieces,
throwing food from the refrigerator on the walls,
lighting fire to the drapes,
but thinking better of that pissing
hard to put the fire out
and make a stench that will have connoisseurs
        of such
                talking for years.

You see, David, I'm worried
you are letting little things
like this distract you
from our art.

Were you as engrossed as you should be
considering the inspiration I've given you,
you would not have noticed
when I appeared naked,
dressed in your clothes,
wrecked your house,
nearly burned it down,
pissed all over creating
an unbearable but,
for those who know
the difference fascinating,
odor that will never leave.

I, on the other hand, will leave forever
unless you give up all allurements
and dwell on the Olympian heights with me,
wholeheartedly engrossed in our art
forever mindful that art is finding
your other half and stitching yourself
back together so you can relax
and enjoy the sweet sweet pleasures,
relax and enjoy the company of the blessed,
relax and enjoy working with the poor,
not as a condescending bitch like me,
but with your own consciousness fully dilated,
relax and enjoy emotional intimacy with all persons,
a close affiliation with all life,
and as you contemplate
material objects, whatever you call them,
you will come to know and love them
as colonies of lost souls.

REGRETS

I'm sorry I cannot commit to your proposed planning meet-
ing.
I'm tied up with what's going on at the Brooklyn Bridge
Owner's Assoc.
Our organization has grown tremendously.
These people are unable to stop talking when others are talk-
ing.
They all must have their say and cannot listen.

Yes, and we will have a big book sale, and we
will sell all the books, and when people ask whom they
should pay,
we will say they can pay anyone, anyone at all, because that
is the way things are done, and if they don't like the way
things are done,
they can take their problem to the United Nations.

MY QUESTION FOR TOM

A man once asked
with a tone of dismay,
"So what's this I hear,
another birthday?"

I landed a punch
square on his nose,
and down he went
for the count in repose.

Then hoisting myself
by my own petar,
I decided to do
something out pretty far.

I wrote me a poem
full of wit and derision
denouncing old farts
who ask for precision.

I told them off good.
I told them off true.
So tell me, dear Tom,
just how old are you?

WHAT MUST BE SAID

Experience is to be kept
retained refined
amalgamated mutated
rehearsed hidden
marinated restrained
redressed revised
falsified commoditized
purified rarefied
reified classified

only then will some
stray vapors escape

to waif their way to
the clouds of the gods.

BROWNING

We six take our seats
in the Cloister of the Clasped Hands,
a room filled with sweat
as the last chairs arrive,

floor sitters assume their positions
around the huge walnut table, larger
than the one owned by Pen Browning,
taking as much space as fourteen of us.

Our host enjoins us not to use cell phones,
and there is no danger
the two-ton bronze chandelier decorated
with bells and pomegranates will fall.

After some Irish
humor about a priest
buying a dog,
he informs us

Paul Muldoon
exceeds all honors
resists all stereotypes
rhymes in mysterious,
amusing ways
has written more sonnets than
any other person alive
considers experience
without limit
like William James
a web like art
in the mind of the producer
on whom nothing is lost.

Paul Muldoon stands before us now,
forty feet from the ceiling above,
telling us he will read
for fifty minutes,

and we should know,
what he only just learned,
after years of using the phrase
without knowing

"forlorn hope"
refers to attackers who make
the first charge to trigger
the defenders initial volley
giving the main storming party
full twenty seconds
to climb the breach
before the defenders
can fire musket or cannon again.

They are the lost heap,
so soldiers more valued
are rejected for such service.

Paul talks and talks
flipping here and there
in his shiny black spring binder,
he talks of rowing toward this country

for fifty years, his soft and halting
voice filling the void above the 200
who occupy this forty-foot square cube
with acoustics than which none better
are known on earth.

Turn on your cell phones, he says,
after a few nature, pet, roadway
and sight-seer bits,
this next one is all about noise,

and from noise we move to soccer moms,
Bob Dylan and that the next poem
was written last year for his sister,
who died of cancer last week,

and that we all must read a wonderful
new book The Irish Hedge School and its Books,
and how at some event or other
at least they weren't speaking French.

Ireland, we learn,
is a place where language
is unrelated to reality,
and, he wants us to know,
some poems about boredom are boring,
every resort is a last resort
and every slope is slippery.

Wave after wave of platitudes
ordered and reordered take us
well beyond the fifty minutes
out to almost an hour,

until the waves of platitudes
are followed by waves of applause,

and wishing the torrent of words
would go on the audience rises as one

not to deliver ovation standing
so much as to mob the man for autographs
before he goes to service
the sales booth in the lobby.

THINGS TO TALK ABOUT ON A DATE

Sew on as so the net is made, and so
the web becomes. Some say make new, indeed
we must, but first make long and larger still.

Encompass, as you spin your words,
the body like a dress.
There's no hiding here;
we all can see
the only poems worth public reading
are those most personal,
read with fear and trembling.

It's one thing to agree
to open up
and play the fool,
quite something else to do it
and survive.

Tell the young not to write;
we've too many poets already.

The great need now is readers please;
they also serve who listen.

WORDS' CALLING

When they talk about word pictures
and tell us how to make it new

seeing objects as spots of color
and feeling alone in the dim light,

there's always more to tell than see
and always more to see than seen,

one never knows when light will fade
or memory fail for the right, just word,

but just as objects persist unobserved,
so words stand ready to hold the thought

prepared.

"The first thought is often the best."
(Bishop Butler, Sermon on the Character of B   am)

FIRST THOUGHT, BEST THOUGHT.

Research on the beat revolution
in religious thought.

Viva la beat! Viva la beat!

Revolution in beat research.

Never look back.
Never look ahead.
Never look!

Jack Kerouac transcribed his life
that we might have life.

Allen Ginsberg used his prophetic imagination
so we could see a new way,
without looking!

Dead beats

Live beats

Go Beats!!!!!!!!!!!!!

Grow beets

Eat beets

Eat big round red healthy beets
And you will be a big round red healthy beat.

APPROACH

our approach is sensual expressive
      not   intellectual
            not   dissective
                   not   explanatory

we are personal reactive
      not   academic
            not   normative

our group is collegial
      not didactic
            cooperative
                 not competitive

what matters becomes
      extent of experience
            immediacy of experience
                 experience with life
                      experience with lived
                         experience

balance integrative and alienative
      balance conventional and idiosyncratic
            balance perennial and apocalyptic

canonical reading presumes M is perfect
      canonical reader never gives up on perfection
            canonical colleague sees perfection
                 perfection refracted in other readers

only if readers are expressive sensual
      do they have the experience of reading
            not the experience called reading
                  reading as central, as demanding priority

reading texts
      that bear the weight of scrutiny
            texts that pay
                  big dividends as life goes on

GROWING OLD ABSURD

Dying more than growing, limbs useless, digits immobile,
no feeling, breath constricted, no pain, mind active, lucid,
as I lie dying, memory alone survives, and desire, desire
to remember and that memory cohere.

I'd been living this terrific comedic poem all my life,
only now with no one to hear and no way to write,
perhaps you have had the same thought—you are not
          reading
this poem, as I lie dying in my home-made hospice—
living will, living well, living by proxy—who the fuck knows?

Even if this goes on a day or so no one will come round
unless I call, which I won't now that I'm warming to this
          death
by dying. So long as memory cooperates, I'd rather go on my
                    own,
the perfect suicide, bound to be listed as paralytic
asphyxiation.

See those toy soldiers? My life on parade.
my fingers are useless now to move them,
if I push them with a pencil I will only make a mess.

So the parade must rest the way it is,
and when I am gone someone will take them away
unaware of what they mean and how my memories cohere
—but what's the harm in that?

MY FINAL OFFER

Self-deception is easy, for something impossible.

Lying reveals more than truth-telling.

For every truth there are many lies.

The lie does not lie; what conceals cannot be concealed.

Tell me your best lies; tell me the lies you love.

ON WHAT WE WERE LOOKING FOR

Remember how you used to sip wine
while the bard recited with rhythm of consequence,
sitting engrossed until rosy fingered dawn joined you
for the last few adventures?
Remember when, on a visit to Turkey,
you did something you should not have done anywhere
and ended up in a dark, smelly room with people
who made you uncomfortable?
Remember your first day of serious shoplifting,
how good it felt to get so much stuff for free
and have the raw balls to go back to the store
wearing the very stuff you had lifted?
Remember your first death,
how cold you were,
how happy and sad at the same time,
how excited you were to tell all your friends
that all and all, worms and all,
death is not that bad?
Even if your memory is less robust,
you can cut it with this crowd
as long as you fail to bore us,
pose no threat of going over the time-limit,
say whatever it takes so when people leave
they feel they have sipped wine with Homer,
beat the system, and lived
many lives eager for many more.